Pebble® Plus

A Visit to
The Doctor's Office

Revised Edition

Download the
Capstone 4D app
for additional content.

 See page 2
for directions.

by Blake A. Hoena

CAPSTONE PRESS
a capstone imprint

Download the Capstone 4D app!

- Ask an adult to search in the Apple App Store or Google Play for "Capstone 4D".
- Click Install (Android) or Get, then Install (Apple).
- Open the app.
- Scan any of the following spreads with this icon:

When you scan a spread, you'll find fun extra stuff to go with this book! You can also find these things on the web at www.capstone4D.com using the password: **doctor.08277**

Pebble Plus is published by Capstone Press,
1710 Roe Crest Drive, North Mankato, Minnesota 56003
www.mycapstone.com

Library of Congress Cataloging-in-Publication Data
is available on the Library of Congress website.

ISBN 978-1-5435-0827-7 (library binding)
ISBN 978-1-5435-0839-0 (paperback)
ISBN 978-1-5435-0867-3 (ebook pdf)

Editorial Credits
Sarah Bennett, designer; Tracy Cummins, media researcher;
Laura Manthe, production specialist

Photo Credits
Capstone Press: Gary Sundermeyer, Cover Left, 7, 11, 13, 17,
19; Getty Images: Thomas Barwick, 15; iStockphoto: andresr,
21, fotografixx, 9, RichLegg, 5; Shutterstock: amirage, Design
Element, PhotoSerg, Cover Background

Note to Parents and Teachers

The A Visit to set supports national social studies standards
related to the production, distribution, and consumption
of goods and services. This book describes and illustrates
a doctor's office. The images support early readers in
understanding the text. The repetition of words and phrases
helps early readers learn new words. This book also introduces
early readers to subject-specific vocabulary words, which
are defined in the Glossary section. Early readers may need
assistance to read some words and to use the Table of Contents,
Glossary, Read More, Internet Sites, Critical Thinking Questions,
and Index sections of the book.

Printed in the United States of America.
010767S18

Table of Contents

The Doctor's Office

A doctor's office is a busy place to visit. People go to the doctor's office when they are sick or need a checkup.

People sit in the waiting room.

They wait to see

a doctor or a nurse.

Around the Office

Office workers keep records and make appointments. They file charts and answer the phones.

Nurses help patients get ready
to see a doctor.
Nurses write down how
much each patient weighs.

Doctors write prescriptions
and read charts.

The Exam Room

Patients see their doctor

in the exam room.

The patient sits on a table

during an exam.

Instruments help doctors

and nurses check their patients.

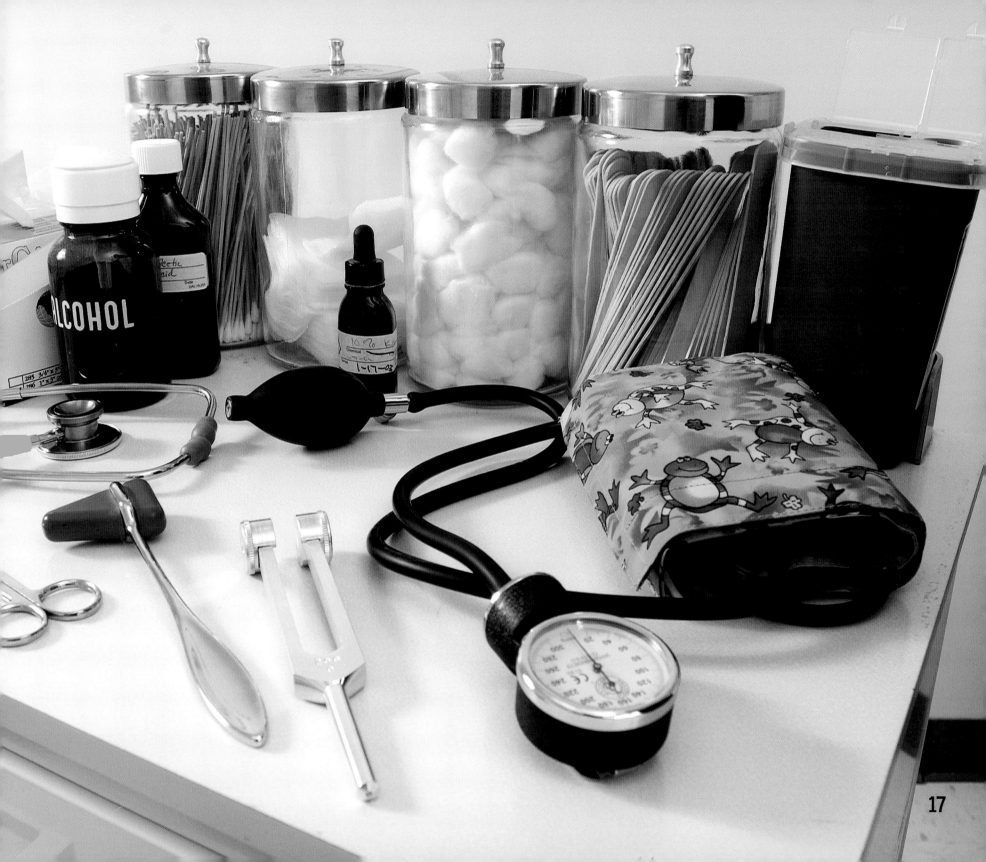

The Lab

Lab workers do tests in the lab.
Gloves keep their hands
clean and safe.

19

Staying Healthy

People visit the doctor's office
to help them feel better
and stay healthy.

Glossary

appointment—an arrangement to meet someone at a certain time

chart—the place where information about a patient is kept; information is added to a chart each time a patient visits the doctor's office

exam room—a room where doctors and nurses check the health of a patient; another word for exam is examination

instrument—a medical tool used to examine or treat patients

lab—a room with equipment that is used to do scientific tests; another word for lab is laboratory

patient—a person who is cared for by a doctor or a nurse

prescription—a written order for medicine

Read More

Bellamy, Adam. *This Is My Doctor.* All About My World. New York: Enslow Publishing, 2017.

Kenan, Tessa. *Hooray for Doctors!* Hooray for Community Helpers! Minneapolis: Lerner Publications, 2018.

Siemens, Jared. *The Doctor.* People in My Neighborhood. New York: Smartbook Media, Inc., 2018.

Internet Sites

Use FactHound to find Internet sites related to this book.

Visit *www.facthound.com*

Just type 9781543508277 and go.

 **Super-cool stuff!** Check out projects, games and lots more at **www.capstonekids.com**

Critical Thinking Questions

1. What do lab workers wear to stay safe?

2. Describe what nurses do.

3. Do you like going to the doctor's office? Why or why not?

Index